Dedicated to my Lord and Savior, Jesus Christ, and my children Amaya and Micaiah.

Shield
of
Faith

This is our belief that Jesus will do what He says He will do and protect us from all the bad things that the enemy tries to do.

Daniel used his faith to believe that God would not let anything happen to him in the lions den.

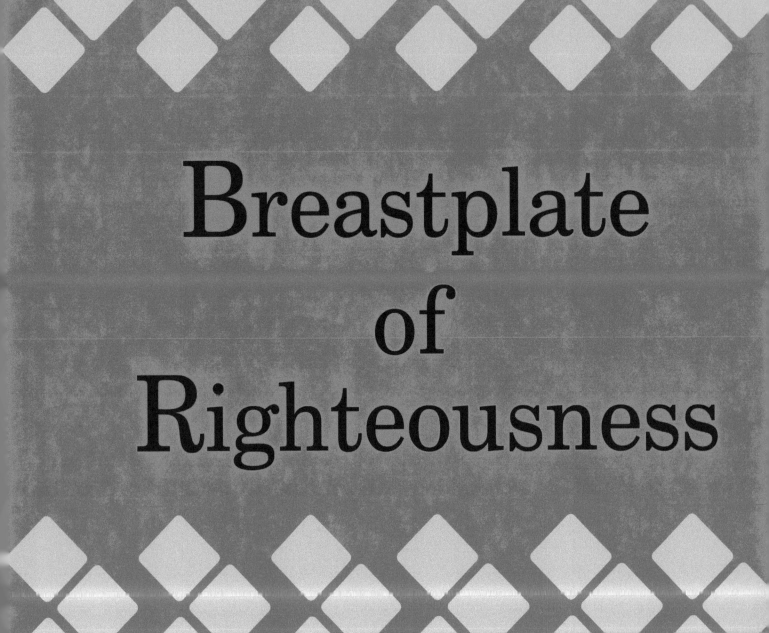

Breastplate
of
Righteousness

Protects our heart by confessing any sin we have, or saying sorry to God for things we've done wrong.

Jonah was swallowed up by a whale for not listening to God's instructions. After God rescued Jonah he realized that he should have listened to God from the beginning.

Helmet
of
Salvation

Protects us from bad thoughts that the enemy tries to put in our mind.

Hannah put her trust in God when she couldn't have a baby. She did not listen to the lies that the devil was telling her. Instead she prayed and God answered her prayer.

Belt
of
Truth

Reminds us that we must always tell the truth no matter what.

Queen Esther saved a lot of people from being killed. She risked her life by telling King Xerses the truth about a situation. She was very brave.

Sword of the Spirit

Represents the Bible we read. By remembering God's word we will be able to tell what is good and what is bad.

Jesus, God's son, was being tempted by the sneaky devil. He tried to trick Jesus but he couldn't because Jesus knew God's word.

Sandals
of
Peace

Helps us become ready to go wherever God leads us and that he will always keep us safe and peaceful when we go.

David defeated
Goliath the giant
because he knew
God was with him
wherever he went
and would never
let him fail.

PRAYER

We communicate with God through prayer. We pray by asking God to put on our spiritual armor to protect us and our family from the enemy.

Together We can win the battle against good and evil through prayer.